One man's journey into the mystic.

INTO THE NOW

ARCH COWAN JONES

Illustrations by Isaac Stone

CONTENTS

Preface / 1

1. Image and Likeness / 5
2. Just What Is / 8
3. Withins / 11
4. In You… I AM… / 13
5. The Shape of Life / 15
6. Blue Jays / 17
7. Worries of the World / 21
8. Buffalo / 24
9. Oak Box / 26
10. Allison's Tree / 28
11. Passing Days / 31
12. Fireworks / 34
13. "We Got to Stay Four Days" / 36
14. Work Shoes / 40
15. How will it look to see us eat in the future? / 42
16. Tracking Solo / 46
17. After Beating COVID / 49
18. Vehicular Egoicide / 51
19. A Modern Fairy Tale / 54
20. "… Ah, so. How can I help?" / 56
21. Let's talk about Oneness / 58
22. Mirror Energy / 62
23. Our Ancestor's Hell / 63
24. AMBER ALERT / 66
25. 'Sin' / 68

26. The Damned Ego Tree / 73
27. My Generation / 79
28. COVID / 83
29. Undying and Unborn / 88
30. The Precipice / 91
31. What If? / 94
32. New Skin / 96
33. Polar Breeze / 100
34. This game we keep playing / 102
35. Attachment / 104
36. Our Destiny / 105
37. Everything is True / 107
38. A Practice / 109
39. Transcending the Temporal / 112
40. The Sam's Wholesale Church / 114
41. The Threshing Floor / 116
42. Humorous Diversity / 118
43. The Universe is Breathing Me / 120
44. Divided Lines / 122
45. 'It'… is Happening / 122
46. The Physicist's Key / 127
47. There is something made of Love up next. / 130
48. God Saves Through Self Emptying / 134
49. Consciousness and… / 138
50. Miracles / 140
51. Home Grown / 144
52. Into the Now / 146

*The nature of infinity is this: That everything has its
own vortex. And when once a traveller thro' Eternity
has passed that Vortex, he perceives it roll backward behind
his path, into a globe itself unfolding; like a sun...
... Thus is the heaven a vortex pass'd already, and the earth
a vortex not yet pass'd by the traveller thro' Eternity.
- William Blake, Milton, 1757-1827*

To my children.

PREFACE

My name is Arch Cowan Jones and my 40th trip around the sun concluded with the onset of the drama that was 2020. A year filled with challenges and realizations. And 2020 found me living as much more of the problem than the solution. My experience of "life" occurred as a child of the United States of America. I grew up in the foothills of the Appalachian mountains with the 1980's and 1990's as my formative years. Life in America during these times could be characterized by expansion, unbridled growth, and competitive striving. Our society is steered by a competitive worldview impressed upon the citizenry for generations. The System conditioned us to strive. Beginning with our educational systems to our youth sports, and later the institutions of power and industry literally fueled by the duality of both scarcities and excesses. My early years reflected these times.

As the lockdowns of 2020 set in, I met the event as a challenge, and I thrive in challenges. I threw myself into a season of self-defense training, physical fitness, dietary and immune system optimization, emersion in nature, and "one more shot" at the "spiritual life" (whatever that means). As part of these pursuits, I spent many hours reading, thinking, walking in forests, walking in the mountains, and many hours sitting in a particular spot in a field, and on one particular rock ledge on the side of a mountain.

I stumbled into what I later learned was sometimes called contemplative meditation, or better yet call it the path of the mystic. It was a season of life filled with whirlwinds of realization and experience, but one epiphany dominated all others…

It is all One. Ultimately, there exists Ontological Oneness.

I don't know if it is most accurate to say that I saw this, as in a vision? Or did I experience a shift in consciousness, or have a realization? Is this what they call transcendence? Or did 'God' speak to me from the 'heavens'? I did not spend much effort in labeling but threw myself into an all-out sprint in the direction of an undeniable pull of truth growing from within my chest.

This endeavor was certainly multifaceted, and part of the work included journaling, writing, and later the words that will fill the pages to follow. I clearly felt a call to the adventure and the challenge of this personal journey. But I also felt called to create this unifying map of words. Conceptual arrows pointing towards this one unifying perennial wisdom as if to say "Meaning… is that way.".

I deeply studied this hypothesis through the vantage point of various related subjects, religions, and diverse fields of wisdom. It was a quest to communicate this same message from the perspective of the other lenses looking into our deepest realities.

My teachers were experts from any discipline I could unearth attempting to answer related questions including physicists, sages, prophets, mystics, poets, historic religious orders, indigenous wisdom traditions, gurus, the lot. If Ontological Oneness was true… I would find it everywhere, and I did. It would be the end of every path, and it was. It would prove to be the underpinnings of ancient faiths, experiential spiritual practices, and the reality on the tip of the tongue of modern thought leaders.

Earth, at the dawn of the year 2020 was in a nose-dive spiral towards countless extinction events and possible planetary death. That remains unchanged as I type these words.

Earth's present predicament is magnified by large scale abandonment of religion turned business and an increasing idolization of technology. Humanity has rapidly lost 'meaning'. And from that consciousness the human experiment seems to be collectively manifesting "Just What is" largely from reactive unconscious conditioning. Human decisions are decimating Earth based on the programming and the demands of established power systems increasingly uncoupled from the heart of what it means to be human. So, ever benevolent, the Cosmos gifted Earth the years 2020 and following as the opportunity to alchemize a pandemic, political and economic turmoil, wars, racism, injustice, and electronic-rage.

Life issued mankind a wakeup calling of experience as the gift of "Just What Is". And Now… is that blessed moment when Earth collectively realizes the manifesting influence We have, in and as each present moment. Before it is too late.

My hope is that in the words that follow we together experience "Just What Is" in a way that brings us individually and collectively present. To be still and as Fr. Rohr says take "a long loving look at the Real".

If you are moved by these words or if the Spirit calls to mind a friend or two as you read I humbly ask that you purchase additional copies of this book and give them away. And please share freely the audio accompaniment to this book, the recordings of the "Into the Now" podcast.

The present moment is the work.
So, I punched in for a double.
The words to follow are what I learned.
And I begin by acknowledging my defeat.
I was not a poet nor a sage.
These words came to me
pretty much this way.
Please accept this as my apology
hard truths like these
words will prove inadequate to convey.
How I found heaven hiding in the now
and Christ consciousness was the way.

1. Image and Likeness

We are made in the "Image and Likeness"* of God.
What are we supposed to do with that?
To live into it, live underneath it,
the pressures of it clinging to our back?

Image is Life. And Life's Spirit is eternal.
As Christ self-empty's the universal consciousness
of each and every One.
The same life, the source, the essence
that compels a flower to stretch.
Offering praise to its sun.

Image is a product of our
Mother's very breath.
Ever expanding, ever donating,
presencing forth through
life and death.
Thus, 'to Be' – defines
'What Is' – as image.
To be image… is just, to Be.
Image is the unified field of This.

As 'thisness' is God's very image
Humans, stones, trees, and birds.
Why then have our religions
become just a squabble over words?
All that is... is God's image.
So, we are all truly One.
We must be present to
'Just What Is' with that as purpose.
Or blindly chasing preferences
into extinction mankind will run.

Likeness though is different;
likeness allows humanity to play the tone.
Consciousness a lifelong project
building a rocket to take us home.
Likeness grows as we surrender
into the infinite unknown.
Death then ignites a homing beacon,
careening back to our Creator's throne.

Our choices then become our likeness
Likeness grows as a flower mirroring the sun.

Will we continue to grow into illusory egos?
Or grow into the consciousness of One?

Image and Likeness... how do we live it well?
Through cul de sacs and finish lines,
only time will tell.
Will mankind honor Image and Likeness?
God... within *All* life!
Seek "the kingdom of heaven"**
and lay aside egoic-strife?

To Image. And to Likeness,
in human beings... should become verbs.
Religion... the single seed that perished
was buried by idolized words.
Now instead Christ grows
from within my chest.
Not just in 'heaven up above'.
As in Me
We
live out the verb
Love.

* *Genesis 1:26*
** *Jesus of Nazareth, Matthew 10:7*

2. Just What Is

Somewhere on the road to 'What Must Be'
is this rocky shore we're standing on;
they call this place – 'Just What Is'.
But when folks swim out-into the ocean
of pasts and futures,
under patterned waves
of illusion they often drown.
Until the Cosmos calls them back,
to wake up, to 'live up', to turn around.

They say right here's the only spot
where you can glimpse infinity.
So breathe in deep. Be here. Be now.*
See the horizon of the cosmic-sea.

If you look deep you can just make it out
as living water pours fresh from the spout.

When you calm your breathing, calm your vision,
you can see What Must Be's horizon.
People say it looks like a mirror,
a sort of holograph of heaven.

And it's always reflecting here and now,
earth and humans, and all our weapons.
Still yet, What Must Be
is growing wild. Growing from this moment.
Out of a single thread of 'now's'
the 'future' will be what Our now's have woven.

Consider what we are doing to the animals,
to the soil, and to the oceans.
Is it not clear to everyone now
that separate ego-consciousness
is irrevocably broken?

And in that breaking we have access
to a change of Being, change of motive, change of skin.
Humanity pouring loving-awareness** into each moment
and just like that... Christ comes again.

A re-membering. A re-ligioning.
A re-ceiving of all 'Just What Is's'.
It's time to lay down these 'separate-selves'
and get on with heaven's unifying business.

Wake up. Breathe in deep. Look and see.
Just What Is, is smack dab in the middle
of the road to What Must Be.
Could a clearer view of this timeless Unity
usher in the Spirit to set us free?

Free to try. Free to hope.
Free to go "Live up Rastaman,
Rastaman live up."***
Drink deep this living water
flowing from What Is's cup.

*Ram Dass, mantra (1931-2019)
**Ram Dass, mantra (1931-2019)
***Bob Marley and the Wailers, "Rastaman Live Up" Tuff Gong 1978

3. Withins

I heard a prophet's song
and it inspired me to sing.
He sang to;
"The one who holds the sun's fire".
He asked "How am I to describe
the one who holds the sun's fire?"*

We describe God in our Being.
As life stretches back into glory.
We are described as God's breath
in our shared religious stories.
Yet Ontological Oneness seems to solve all of the riddles,
eases burdens, changes yokes,
inspires charity, big and little.

I sought out God's face,
and God showed me
all my friends.
God is not without,
God is not other,
but is patiently waiting within our withins.

'Science' and 'religion' now sing the same tune
though they refuse to listen.
God is pouring out God
as moments of existence for us to Christen.

What is this all about? Life!?!?
And why does suffering get to join us?
And when will kenotic-love
again become humanity's chorus?

I sought God...
and God showed me all my friends.
And gave me eyes so I could see
the fractals of God within Withins.

*Trevor Hall, "31 Flavors", Trevor Hall 2009.

4. In YOU... I AM...

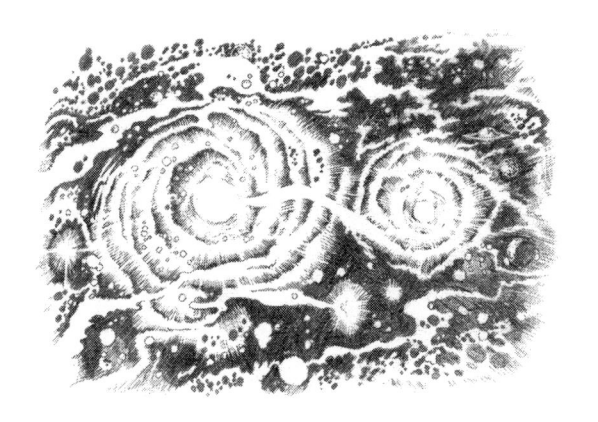

As the word of God thunders forth,

it creates a resounding chorus.

God's-breath rending life

from the quantum's potential

obviously does not happen quietly.

Matter Being birthed

as darkened vacuum spins

into bright consciousness!

Our Creator has an echo,

it's God's resonance in Us.

But we then stumble out from birth

as servants of misplaced worth.

Awareness trampled by the 'mind',
entranced so fast by 'space' and 'time'.
We learn worldly games and
some of us learn how to win.
But the ante for that table
is a spirit scraped too thin.

Awakening though is realizing
we ourselves we are God's breath.
Word poured into matter;
and we blew along as what was left.
We are not just our thoughts
or the egos never-ending monologue.
Yet consciousness is being lost in a meme of
'self-hood' like a-boiling-pot-of-water-frog.
Pure awareness though is free to love Just What Is,
not just the preferences of the mind.
Consciousness does not breathe
and is not bound by 'space' and 'time'.

Jesus Christ showed the path
when the cup He would not pass.
I'll try to reverberate that cadence,
till in YOU… I AM… at last.

5. The Shape of Life

We all know a one-dimensional reality is a myth.
And two dimensions..? That doesn't make sense at all.
Three dimensions are too often mankind's top floor.
But I've heard there's something like
9 dimensions or more
described by philosophers and psychedelic explorers.

I have come to see that each moment
is a point inside of a fractal.
A meta-dimensional toroidal fractal.
The cosmic umbilical cord of God.
And this very moment. This one...
is just an energetic node or a pod.

You and I, each play a uniquely necessary role.
In realizing glory, life to the full, right here and now!
To walk the path of Christ.
Is to turn the other cheek.
Smile into the teeth of the scowls.

To seek the kingdom of heaven
in this moment's abundance,
whether joy or suffering compels.
Is to lay aside attachments, distractions,
separate ego-consciousness.
And conjure up no more of our own hells.

So, the shape of life, heaven
takes form as we realize and allow
the 'kingdom of heaven'
to be made of 'Just What Is'.
In smiles and tears. Joy and sadness. Here and now.
Blood sweat across the Christ's brow.*
The meta-dimensional fractal reDivinizing of matter
we experience it… in forms. In life and in death.
But eternity is a fractal, a ladder.
In what's given here and now each next breath.

*Luke 22:44

6. Blue Jays

Bruce Springsteen once sang
"if you've ever seen a one-legged man...
you've seen me."*

Well, I once saw a family of blue jays,
some bound to the ground.
Some flew on the breeze through the trees.

And I saw ants too.
Ants always seem so destructive.
But not nearly as destructive as man.
Is earth now treating us humans?
The same way I treat an invading ant-clan?
To protect my home, I get out the TERRO.
Is Mother Earth... getting out Her Raid?
Because She's tired of being exploited for 'likes',
tired of this egoic consumerism charade?

You see these two blue jays
seem to have been born missing tail-feathers.
Or maybe all blue jays are born this way?
Maybe they all develop sheltered under tables?
As they await tail feathers, to then fly away.
Do all young blue jays hide away on homeowner's patios?
And do all their parents, and all their parent's friends
scream into defensive positions from the trees
as they descend?

Dive bombing the man who lives there.
Protecting awkward, fragile, overgrown chicks
from this human and all of his cares.

To be fair I did once relocate one of these
adolescent birds to the lawn
using the back of a chair.
But that was before...
of this whole blue jay fiasco, I became aware.
I just acted on dumb-instinct like a dare
Gotta fix the problem,
get the blue jay up and out of there.
Our patio doesn't even have stairs.

But up in the trees when I sat to meditate about 2:00.
I came to learn these two hopping,
squawking, no tail-feathered jays
had a crew. They came out of the blue.
Seemed like nothing they wouldn't do.
Blue jays buzzing my ears and then flying away.
At that moment, all I could do, was what I set out to do.
Pray.
Intending to influence the energy
of our shared environment.
And undo the threat they saw in me.
Breathe some peace up into the air
and from panic let peace set them free.

I prayed "God, help the blue jays with no tail feathers.
And those with wings... busy protecting them too."
Who knows what's blowing in on this weather?
It's gonna take a miracle
for us jays to make it through.
And with that the volume did actually dim.
The protective jays settled onto their limbs.

Breathing In: I relaxed body and mind.
Breathing Out: I enjoyed a smile.
Breathing In: I am present... no more grind.
Breathing Out**: I am in awe of eternity growing wild.

*Bruce Springsteen, "The Wrestler", Working on a dream 2008.
** Thich Nhat Hanh, (a paraphrasing) Peace is every step, Bantam Books 1991.

7. Worries of the World

I yelled out "I love you!"
to my wife while brushing my teeth the other day.
She was headed out to pick-up our son,
down the stairs she walked away.
I hate that I do this, but I immediately fretted,
"how did that land?"
This compulsion, to think the worst
to worry she's mad – and to start to plan.

Internally projecting potential failures
has always been my instinct.
Spin up a mental worst case
then worry out ways to protect against it.

Instead of picturing her smiling
assuming, she's thinking fondly of me.
That my verbal gesture landed softly,
that her offer, to cover pickup
was a gift. And she gave it for free.

Then again the next morning I had a fright
stepping out the back door.
I thought I locked myself – outside
at five-something in the morning.
Frantically I reached back for the door in utter panic!
I just locked myself – outside,
everyone is asleep... Damnit!
Just to realize that of course the door was still un-locked.
Adrenaline though... had already flooded my chest,
Heart,
Reeling,
Shock.

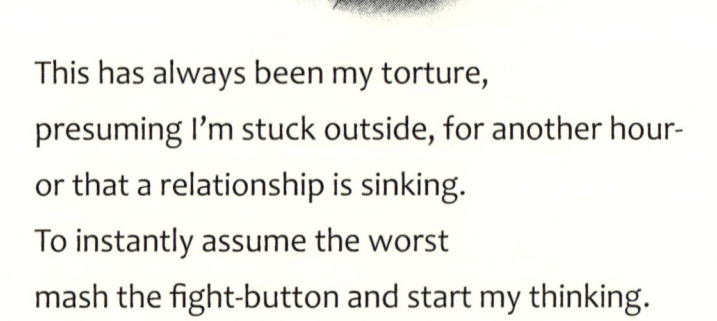

This has always been my torture,
presuming I'm stuck outside, for another hour-
or that a relationship is sinking.
To instantly assume the worst
mash the fight-button and start my thinking.

There's a problem, and no one else to help
everyone-else is soundly sleeping.

I wonder, am I alone,
or do others face this battle?
Or am I being way too honest?
Of our neuroses, should we not tattle?
At this point in the journey,
I'm not into holding back.
In hopes next time that I'll remember,
and not give in, to the lie... of lack.

Could I find a new rhythm?
Where I always assume the best.
Stay present to Just What Is.
And take it easier on my chest.
No longer consumed by fears and emotions
the lies that ego conditioning
constantly hurls.
But instead live a life of hope.
Live "in the world,
not of the world."*

*Jesus of Nazareth, John 17:14-18

8. Buffalo

Buffalo run headlong into storms.
Fear is not conditioned, as a buffalo's norm.
And likewise, when learning to ride a bicycle,
you can't save your day by turning the wheel away,
away from crashing into the painfully physical.
But you must steer the front-wheel
toward impending falls.
Sorta like Dante and Virgil's epic crawl.
Down through the belly of satan was their way outta hell.

Lao-Tzu spoke of water eternally seeking the quantum.
Jesus Christ poured out moments as servant of all.
He taught to be the guest who sits first at the bottom
before being raised up, raised up to the head of the hall.

Or take the example of driving
through a winter snow storm,
when tires slide, and the back end loses grip.
Control returns by steering into the drift.
Heaven's construction could require another
sixty decimal orders of magnitude. Or it could be swift.

But, to run into... that storm.
Will require a planetary consciousness shift.
Or the competition over separate preferences
will be realized as our existential cliff.

Unless We now. Each turn-around,
unite in love by transcending the egoic mire.

But from here and now...
that'd all be quite a feat.
This game of 'otherness' is coming down to the wire.

A Buddha was once asked;
"How may we escape this brutal heat?"
He said, "there is freedom... in the heart of the fire."

*Thanks to the collective teachings of – Alan Watts, Rich Froning, Dante Alighieri, Lao-Tzu, Jesus Christ, Nassim Haramein, Mother Nature, Boyd Varty, James Finley, and the Buddhas.

9. Oak Box

Spirit shared with me a picture of an oak box.
Not a box that closes, it had no hinges... had no locks.
This box it sat wide open. A capacity to be filled.
But all that fits within it,
is what's been given, not what's been willed.

This box once stood as a tree.
Living, breathing, into the sky.
But whether axe, or saw, or age
all that breathes will one day die.
This box is me. I am this box,
as far as purpose goes.

In three dimensions I am alive.
But this form will not survive,
and I already feel the curtains start to close.

The box too once lived,
and yet now remains a capacity for others.
Humanity's purpose is to grow open
to all that Just What Is uncovers.

What is man?
But destined, to one day once have been.
And what s God? But all that Is.
Our fundamental Fabric and our Friend.
Therefore, while I breathe,
I will make We... the biggest box I can.
An open box not grown from oak,
but from the consciousness of man.

The box was empty of preferences.
It existed in openness, great-big, and wide.
We are destined... to be filled!
And present moments grow taller sides.

10. Allison's Tree

I planted a little tree in the front yard for my wife.
I won't tell her what kind of tree,
no matter what her offering price.
Because this tree was a gift, it was the gift of life.
A cooperation with God, to do something sweet.
I planted a thoughtful-tree you-see
and the dance... is wait and see.
Will it fruit?
Will it flower?
Or will it open up in shade?
To know its fate she'll have to wait,
for that surprise I will not trade.

She'll ask from time to time
"What kind of tree is it"?
I only say... "It's a magic tree".
It'll turn out to be magic
if somehow it survives me.

I saw this little tree.
The biggest of her sisters still left at Kroger.
A limb broke off in the truck.
It jammed into the window driving over.

Digging out an old stump was… fun. I finally managed.
Then tossed in several kinds of dirt.
I had to prune off the limb I damaged
…and that part it kinda hurt.

But amongst the oaks though this tree is tiny!
Is it possible? Could it have shrunk?
It looks more like a stick, hardly passing for a trunk.
It's become just like a playground,
for the neighborhood chipmunks.

My moments as loving caretaker
are as far as I get to go.
Will Allison's tree Christ forth with life?
Or die this winter, I do not know.

Hands dirty, inspecting leaves,
holding a watering can.
I wonder what God sees,
in the limbs and leaves of man?
And does both a 'Divine-will'...
and a 'Cosmic-karma'
steer life's unfolding plan?

I hope we are given
enough time here on Earth
so one day we are blessed to see.
What will be of Our future?
And what will be of Allison's tree?

11. Passing Days

We have a cat named Marley. ☺
She's made of stardust... just like me.
When she talks to me in the morning
I think she knows she's truly seen.
Sort of like my lime trees,
they get stressed.
And they miss their sun.
It all adds up to the same old line.
It is All – truly One.

If Creation could speak to us,
I wonder what it all would say?
The trees, the birds, the fish.
I bet they'd ask us to change our ways.
Because the future we are pursuing
will eventually silence the birds.
And trees will become novelties,
as mechanical lungs breathe our words.

But maybe there's another way.
A way of Being that reconnects us with the Earth.
When we alchemize that "Let there Be",*
breathed the mountains, the streams, you, and me.

No, nature is not "the point"... of life.
This ground is our brother, sister, mother.
Beyond the veil of foolishness,
of treating Her as 'other'...

Human consciousness grew
in a field of spin, we know it as Earth...
way, way, back to times unknown.
But mankind now ravages the soil.
We treat Her as victim... not as Home.

It all goes back to 'otherness'.
The weapon of evil in these present times.
But what do I know..?
I'm sitting in a sunroom
talking to cats and spitting rhymes.

How do I tie this one off?
I'm not sure where this poem's going.
How can Oneness grow from otherness?
Maybe more composting?
And less mowing?

Ok, that line just didn't cut it,
I'll have to think up another.
Earth... is pleading with us
to treat Her more as brother, less as other.

So go outside. Breathe in deep.
Let your conscious presence – run and play.
Because all you've ever truly owned
are present moments, in passing days.

12. Fireworks

Imagine with me for a minute if you will
a ride you could describe as the epitome of a thrill.
Let your memories return to
a great fireworks show.
Screaming out through open skies
fireworks tend to go... just where they go.

Red, white, green, and blue
they stretch out into the night.
Their streaks and movements not criticized.
Not described as wrong, or right.

The Designer fills each shell
with hopes for the show
but the beauty is when they explode,
they tend to go... just where they go.

Though it may seem kinda silly,
I have an analogy to tell.
The Universe as all we know it
is just a cosmic mortar shell.

As God donates God as our experiences
our communities, our friends.
And lights the fuse on Life, while we realize
Pop.
Ride.
End.

But could it be within the show
the sparks could become Conscious?
So that we'd stop inventing 'hells'
and piling them upon us?

Conscious sparks instead would Become!
In accord with diverse Divine design.
Fireworks of consciousness
would be the literal glory-cloud of the Divine.

What if mankind began to see God
as the infinite toroidal mortal shell?
From the quantum to the cosmic
that's the story it all seems to tell.

Fireworks... Well, We...
We tend to go just where We go...
Because We sometimes forget that We...
We... co-create the show.

13. "We Got to Stay Four Days"

"We got to stay four days",
said a girl in braids and bathing suit to me.
I looked back at her and smiled,
we were both on vacations,
and in that moment, we were free!

We had our portion of the good life,
the sun, the sand, the smell of the sea.
Perfectly curated shops and markets,
stretched as far as our eyes could see.

She said, "We get to stay for four days".
And with some sadness she smiled down on me,
from perched atop her Momma's back,
like she was climbing on a tree.

I didn't know how to respond,
my plan – went no further than my smile.
But what fumbled out of my mouth
I wish I thought on for a while.

This girl was 7 or 8, with braided pigtails
tied up with those marble balls.
Her older sister kept her hair natural.
I wish the words I spoke had been
more inspired and less factual.

Because I clumsily said smiling back,
"I think we get to stay four days too".
I'm not even sure on that math,
I didn't take time to think it through.

She seemed well loved. Within a tribe.
Family. Four generations of women
headed home in a cramped-up ride.
To make room they offered me their extra waters,
but I polite-fully declined.
As for bottled waters I too was oversupplied.

But I wonder... if my eyes reflected the sadness
of the vacation ending dismay?
How we all longed for more 'vacation'
free from worry, free from suffering.
Free! For just another day.

There was a sharing in the air
as we were untethered from life's cares.
The weight of those six words
they caught me totally unawares.

After my 'four days' we were all back home
in life as we had known it.
I wish instead, right there, we'd hatched a plan.
Each gone back to a power-system and over-thrown it.
Because Life… should be lived free!

Freed from fear by
Just What Is within the present moment.
Freedom is ours!
It's our preferences…
that make us forget we already own it.
We labor all year long for a couple weeks.
For homes, for stuff, for our "four days".
Human consciousness though
exists to manifest love
not to chase this year's
borrowed clothes and borrowed stays.

I helped the grandmother pack up her tent,
and wished them blessings on their way.
But I can not forget her bittersweet smile
and young voice say...
"We got to stay... four days".

14. Work Shoes

There was dried grass stuck
to the soles of my black work shoes.
And dust all across the toes.
The last time I had them on my feet
I remember those toes
they almost froze.

I helped carry my Uncle Bruce
through the snow to his grave.
Uncle Bruce was a man of the snow,
and wouldn't you know it,
it snowed that day.
It was a swirling, dancing, haze
it was Bruce's goodbye wave.

I pulled them out again today
to say goodbye to Cousin Cal.
Separated by age and health,
but wouldn't you know it, we became pals.
Oh, the evolution of Life
we have lived in these short years.
What we are now living is the fruit
of our collective appetites and fears.

Presently it seems
we're evolving through a collective death.
But with death, new life
as humanity's hope endlessly renews.

Today I slowed down enough to notice
My work shoes had evolved
into funeral shoes.

15. How will it look to see us eat in the future?

"How will it look to see us eat... in the future?"
Was the thought I had
finishing off the last of a protein shake.
Food, after we're forced to realize
that the separateness of ego-consciousness
was the antichrist. Not the goal.
We made a collective mistake.

A future when meat and vegetables
are not plentiful anymore.
Because Corporations and Politicians
once upon a time held the tap wide open, full pour.

Oh, to be truly impoverished. Forsaken.
Living in the West , I don't have a clue.
And that's coming from a kid
whose family needed charity,
handouts, kindness, even food stamps too.

We will all know real poverty in the future,
unless we now radically change.
We like to play pretend that it's not our responsibility
but our consumption pours out suffering like rain.

There are places on Earth where Life
is birth, 'life', and death inside squalor.
The consequence of our demand.
Lives spent sourcing raw materials
for us to chew up and mouth feed
to Facebook, to Twitter, and Instagram…

To the charge of raping once beautiful planet Earth
"The Class of 2020" was found guilty
with blood on our pants.
A windfall verdict of karma is being poured out
onto the faces of the children of man.
Present and future suffering is our fruit.
Look now, sorrow is growing.
Growing from inside our hands.

In the future I wonder how it will be
in the affluent West when we finally see.
When we weep at the roots,
eating the fruit
that only grows on the limbs of barren trees.

To actually know
the sights, smells, and tastes,
to go with the names of Earth's fabled fruit.
Our descendants will only dream at the chance.
Real fruit would be considered
the height of rare decadence.

So, I guess I should be happy
if we end up achieving some astronaut type future.
Where we figure out some Matrix* type-shit.
And they chemicalize all our nutrients.
And we 'eat' a man-made-protein-amino-drip.

Eventually… (I thought)
"I guess this is how we'll all eat."

As the bottom of my cup made its crest.
It looked like an oceanic sunset
made out of chocolate-y bliss.
A post-workout kiss on the lips.

But I was saddened by this view of the future.
Of an Earth… with less produce
and more whips.

* *"The Matrix", Lana and Lilly Wachowski 1999.*

16. Tracking Solo

There is a war of consciousness inside my head.
Ever chattering fears and desires
fall on me like a cartoon piano
before I even make it out of bed.

I don't know why I do it
or why it's done to me.
The "knowledge of good and evil"* are my fetters
binding moments... from Being free.
I try to practice loving presence.
And I ask for help along the way.

But it always seems as if I'm told
instead, I should preference
the ideologies that produced these days.
Days marked by strife.
The competition for comforts, modern life.
That's the fruit we are growing
as Human-Beings as the 'Bride of Christ'.
Am I so wrong to long for better???
For a future wholeness for the Earth?

Are We even giving Her a chance?
Or is egoic otherness actively ending
Life's poetic dance?

I saw a path of hope,
the justice of Oneness in the math.
Yet when I try to share this vision
it only seems to elicit orthodoxy's practiced laugh.

Men in positions of power
retreat to established ways,
to positions protected, to the ego's ruse.
Our leaders decisions are compromised
as pride and position they deign not lose.

So, the game of separateness they play
as paths of least resistance become their way.
Maybe not to idols but to ideologies they pray.
Pressing oil from our youth,
commoditizing them,
from the day they are born.
Conditioned... to be used. Wait did I say use?
I meant accuse, misuse, abuse, and then refuse.
Like children sold into slaughter.
No, don't wake up... just keep the car on cruise.

I don't know, what's my point?
The difference I thought that I could make?
All I know is man's current objective,
seems to be to move up the schedule of our wake!

I cannot transplant these eyes to see
or ears to hear – they are mine until I'm dead.
God, my God help me carry the weight
of this dystopian future
waging a war inside my head.

How does this poem land?
Is there any insight here to gain?
I guess once more I must track You solo.

Go back inside
for more words...
and try to better explain.

Genesis 2:9, 2:16-17

17. After Beating COVID

After beating COVID...
Memaw died at 86
of all *other* causes
right before Christmas this year.

I typically feel
mournful tears rise
when a loved one dies.
But today at her burial I could not cry.
Cathartic tears didn't
well up in my eyes.

I guess because I saw it today.
As in far-off.
Memaw's gone somewhere
I soon will follow.
But I don't mean
this same ground
in this same hollow.
But follow her to 'Heaven',

the great cosmic Valhalla.
So, I just stood there
and stared off down the hill.
Remembering fried-chicken,
"boy-fudge", and apple-butter.

Wishing Memaw's heart
was still full
of Memaw's flutter.

And we were gathered round
her table for another
famous after church
Sunday-supper.

18. Vehicular Egoicide

Our vehicles are failing us.
They all will be recycled.
All will go to one place,
all are from the dust.
And to stardust they will return.

Our protests have it wrong,
but not in what it is that we believe.
But in winning public vindication
to now become our enemies.
Injustice will not die by abolishing the prisons.
Since exchanging now oppressors for new oppressors
became the goal of our divisions.
As long as our oppressors have their human sacrifice,
they'll force feed us tribal allegiance.
Withering of our shared Spirit is ignorance's price.

Though I'm starting to remember
what I had to once have known.
That in our Oneness there is something,
from Earth's ground was never grown.

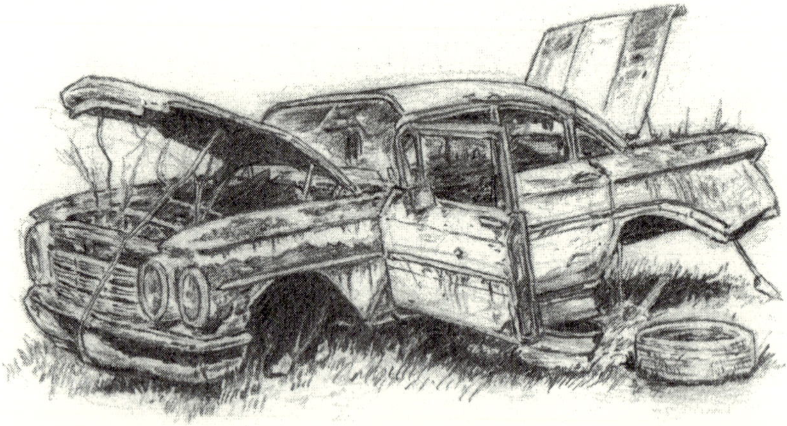

Something different. Something eternal.
Something we've all felt the pull to enter.
God exists, as ALL that Is.
Our Creator is our center.
Though "God's center is everywhere,
His circumference cannot be measured."*
ALL is ONE.
But egos keep us blinded
by the distract-fulness of treasures.
Fooled by the illusions that we...
That 'I' drive the car.
As the left became the right
we crashed headlong with doors-ajar.

It's hard work transcending the otherness delusion
from within vehicles made of future scrap.
But it's time to give up on our idols,
all our preferences are traps.
Jesus Christ pointed the way
to the seed that had to die.
Why am I – just now hearing
"God stopped counting...
and switched sides."?**

*Unknown (various) "The Book of the 24 Philosophers", etc.
** Richard Rohr OFM, "Another Name for Every Thing Podcast".

19. A Modern Fairy Tale

Modern life has become a trippy-ass fairy tale.
With treats and treasures
dropping from the sky by parachute pails.
We're taught to squabble
over scraps and envy fame.
Like castaway children in the Hunger Games.*

Society has conditioned us
to feel stranded and alone.
Left to make it on our own.
But instead of a tropical island
or a mountain forest we...
live at home.
And media polls disclose
we do jobs we loathe
as if we were drones.

But I guess as long as the packages
continue to be delivered to my home.
I'll obey the Politicians
spewing injustice from propped up thrones.
Because, since my prosperity
is up to me you see, I must go along.

I am not free.
So, in that case,
my energy,
shouldn't be,
given free,
...I should... sell it.

Go out into the world dressed just so and dance.
Casting spells, cashing checks,
wondering if I'll ever advance.
It is dizzying. Better yet insane,
this separate competing ego's game.
While corporations literally pay politicians
to keep the game, forever *tilted* just the same.

Beyond dizzying, it aches my brain.
Oh, what could mankind do!
With a good reframe?
Because I believe in Humanity.
The latent Unity forming You and Me.
I believe We are inter-dependent, utterly, thoroughly.
I believe We will one day see
that the ride... to Heaven... was driven by We.

*Hunger Games – Suzanne Collins, 2008. Scholastic Press.

20. "...Ah, so. How can I help?"

The combined mantras
"...Ah, so".* and "How can I help?"**
this morning fell heavy on my heart.
Contemplating the stars from a hammock on the patio,
time spent with the Cosmos is becoming a lost art.

Gravity fools us that we are looking up and not out.
But in reality, we are looking off from Earth's side.
Is Anyone out there hearing our shouts?
Humanity is drowning
in all the ways we divide.

Meditating outside, just before first light.
I realize if we could see *every* star clear,
they would fill up the whole of our sight.
Looking off from the side of the sphere,
makes me wonder
what's the meaning of Our Being here?

Stars, fill the sky as pin holes on a backlit canopy,***
but infinity is infinite in both directions.
And egoic-appetites will remain our collective fantasy,
until we surrender into
the present moment's connections.

Allow those mantras to become an aura, a belt.
And meet moments with "...Ah, so. How can I help?"

* *Zen Master Hakuin (1686-1769) a paraphrasing.*
** *Saint Teresa of Avila (1515-1582) a paraphrasing.*
*** *Incubus, "Wish You Were Here", Morning View, 2002.*

21. Let's Talk About Oneness

'Christians' tend to get squirmy when we
approach the topic of Oneness.
Like it somehow detracts from 'God'
when we transcend the false bravado of 'otherness'.

What is a higher honor than to follow
into God eternally as Spirit leads?
The inevitable singularity of Love
is our destiny!
Whisper the mystics and the trees.

Let's talk this through a little.
None of your beliefs have to change.
Let the grip on ideologies just wiggle.
Let Spirit tell of a faith with some range.

It's hard to argue that 'in Heaven'
we won't be closer.
We will see God… without the veil!
But where does the Almighty's
increased proximity falter?
Where does God's eternal magnetism fail?

They say we will live in His city.
And I can't imagine just what that means?
What is described by "many mansions"*?
Will it be all gold?
Or will it be more green?

But what I really want to know is where I will live?
How close will be my view?
How close will my street be to God's street?
Will we be neighbors?
Or will I have to look for God
over eons of pews?
Will it be just rejoicing souls
lined up the length of galaxies?
Seas of separate Beings all made new?

I believe God's pull is too mighty
and Christ's outpouring love will one day undo
all the separateness life builds up.
In 'Heaven' there'll be no 'view'.

Emersed in a "Christ-soaked existence"**,
without all this illusory game.
No more mobile phones
serving as our prison guards.

Or competitions, over preferences
that've become our chains.

What if we pushed back
from the concept of 'otherness'?
Killed off the ego's pride and joy, the separate-self.
Just allow for the potential of Oneness.
Leave the bailout of individual 'rapture'...
leave it up on the shelf.
And instead receive the call to-together
find solutions
to these problems we collectively caused.
But it becomes increasingly
less likely we'll do it
as long as an eternally
separate self remains involved.

If instead we again see each tree and person
as an extension of a unified-true-self.
Suffering and bitterness will wither
as Christ's-Consciousness grows bigger.
Oh wait, wait... I better slow down.
Tamp down my hope it's easy to trigger.

That I've wasted too much time
without making a point, I'm starting to fear.
And about my disjointed rambles
people will start to talk.

So, I'll conclude by saying;
We need new eyes to see, and new ears to hear
that in Oneness…
God and man do share life's walk.

* *Jesus of Nazareth, John 14:2*
** *Richard Rohr OFM, "The Universal Christ: How a Forgotten Reality Can Change Everything We See, Hope For, and Believe." 2019.*

22. Mirror Energy

Enmity, strife, and turmoil
became the currency of this age.
Modern lives resemble rockets
who refuse to switch their stage.

Back-biting,
growling,
barking

are how packs of dogs relate.
We must now jettison
that tired energy.
And allow Love
instead to radiate.

23. Our Ancestor's Hell

Some things are formed of harder stuff.
Take how storms expose stone to form bluffs.
Tough stuff is not eroded, it endures.
Sheer presence endlessly giving.
As Our spec of space dust keeps on spinning.
Strength, unity, community is and always has been
a prerequisite of earthly living.

Consider even our recent ancestors.
You had to be determined
just to be back then.
A few generations ago –
they didn't even have fans!
It would've been scary hot back then
without a breeze.
And people you knew...
had probably died in a winter's freeze.

Survival required unified
ancestral grit like steel.
For us to have made it
to this point on life's wheel.

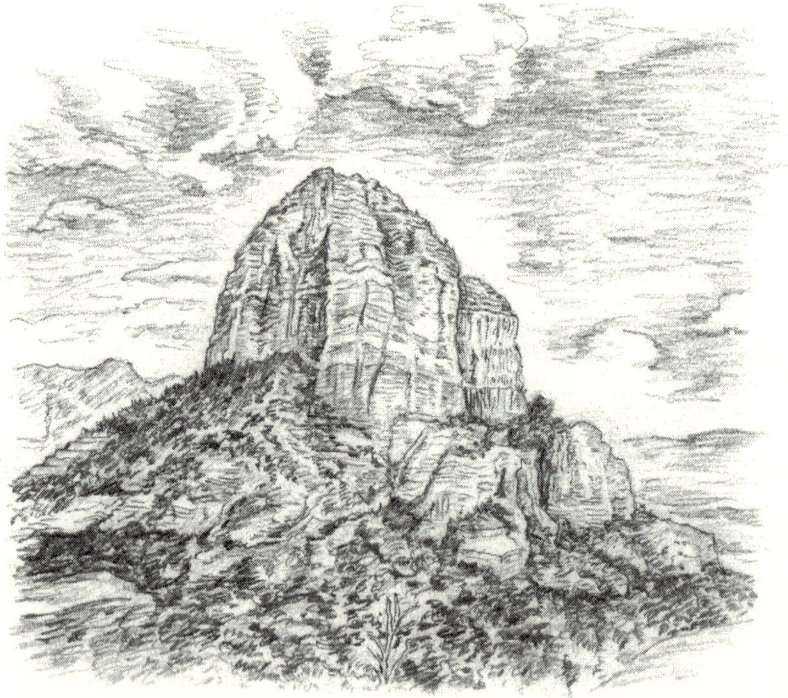

Over-consumption back then was rare.
Our ancestors often ate what was shared.
Now our species staggers
consumed by separate cares.
While media machines tell Us unity
lies broken beyond all repairs.

Or take a sober look at the state of our youth.
A view not of projections but see the truth.
We must be honest,
about the future that now is making.
And the humans we are collectively generating.
Seems to me like fearful egos...
separated into factions of hating.

It sometimes feels like I can hear our elders' wail.
...What would our gangster-ass,
tough as nails ancestors yell?
I bet it'd go something like;
"Be still!"
"Get back to nature!"
"Quit building!"
"What y'all are becoming,
was what we called hell."

24. AMBER ALERT

"A #TNAMBERAlert has been issued
for 2-day old...
(I'm here poetically deleting her real name)
on-behalf of the Memphis Police Dept.
She was last seen
yesterday
in the area of Sedgewick Drive
and Levi Rd in Memphis.
(She) was last seen
wearing a black and white
polka dot onesie with pink pants.
She weighs 6 pounds. And is 17 inches long.
She has brown hair and brown eyes.
If you have seen (her)
or know where she can be found call M.P.D."

...In 2022-going on 2023
oh, the horrors we are causing
as we spin in-to infinity.
Literally hurdling through the cosmos
on a Planck oscillating wave of the cosmic sea.

But here on Earth... searing pain
like we're chasing the sun down the drain.
We've created a world where a girl
at 2 days old
is taken into the cold.

Is she with enemy?
Or with friends?
Or with a trafficking ring
for sale and for spend?
Who takes a 2-day old girl?
From Levi and Sedgewick's corners...
(She) was wearing polka dots,
a onesie
and pink drawers.

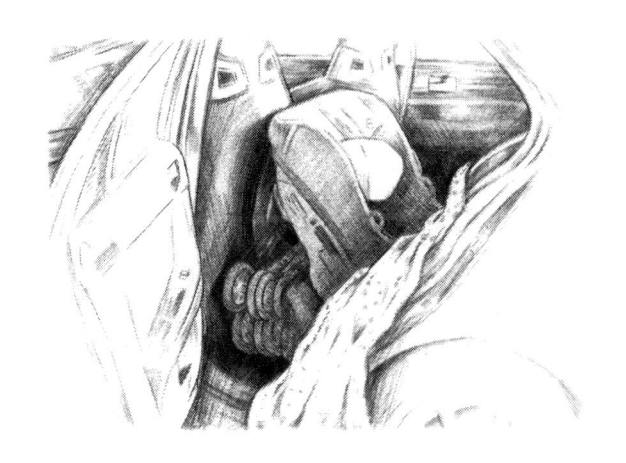

25. 'Sin'

I am beginning to define the word 'sin'
as the "errors that proceed
from perceived separateness".
Again, 'sin' = the error that proceeds
from our mis-perceived separateness.
The prize that ego-consciousness wins
is the piling up of the suffering
of our planet and our friends.
Is there any hope for the oceans,
for the skies, for our neighbors?
And what is the point?
What is our fruit?
What are we birthing from all our labors?

All too often, the emotions of meaning-less-ness rise.
Hope-less. Point-less.
Fears and tears fill Earth's eyes.
We once lived, we'll all die.
Why even waste the time it takes to cry.
Humanity seems to be giving in
to the demon of hope lost.
Manifesting the depth of God's 'benevolence'
has so far required this cost.

Because the summation of our actions
is collective responsibility for 'sin' in the fractions.

And it's starting to seem that to realize
the depth of God's grace
we had to endure the misery of this infernal rat-race.
But does it have to be this way? And how deep will it go?
Well, that's where we come in,
cause it's We who will know.

Currently unconsciousness is steering our ship
habitually directing where we go.
And that's into an ocean of otherness,
as a dark frozen sea.

But I believe one day we will awaken and see
that grace was always the geometry, forming infinity.

Capital L-Love is inevitable.
We cannot outrun it; it will not run dry.
The Christ calls out to stop 'othering',
tend to what is lodged in our own eyes.*

Because we are poisoning our eyes
with the media's lies.
As they pass out labels marked 'other'…

And goad each of us to assign.
To dress up 'others'
in any variety of disguise.
Anything 'other' than me…
looking out from your eyes.
But in truth, we are all Us
looking out from Our eyes.

So, then what is separate ego-consciousness' fruit?
It is the culmination of 'sin's' depravity.
As we are burying ourselves
in this negative energetic gravity.

But since God holds the future
secure in Love's vice.
Then it's our actions, our choices
tabulating 'sin's' price.

Our collective energies
have turned into our cross.
Earth is now wallowing
in man-made suffering and loss.

When will Anthropos return to Consciousness pure?
How much of our filth will the Cosmos endure?
We are currently driven by pride, fears,
and materialistic urges, to own-it.
But 'Life-abundant' is still found
hiding within the present moment.

It's time to wake up.
Become conscious
thoughtfully realize Our role.
It's time we turn round
reduce humanities toll.

In these times we inhabit,
it is time for mankind's rally.
We can each start,
in our spheres as we reshape 'sin's' tally.

The utter pervasiveness of love
has always been Our only hope.
Let Us repent from all this otherness.
There's no end to God's rope.

But what will be the length of 'sin's' epoch?
The span of otherness' years?
Before Cosmic grace as living water,
washes away Earth's
well-earned tears?

* Jesus of Nazareth, Matthew 7:3-5

26. The Damned Ego Tree

Let's revisit a story that's been
passed down through generations.
A story about the dawning
of suffering and of separations.
When 'ego-consciousness'
was born it was first described.
as the fruit of a forbidden tree.

Then separate-selves... hid
behind separate bushes
and separate 'ego's' grew
from the discarded seed.
May I freshen up that allegory?
Speak clearly what I believe?
That under the damned ego tree
we forgot this-nesses inherent unity
in the fabled story, of Adam and Eve.

The setting was a garden
all things
growing forth
naturally.

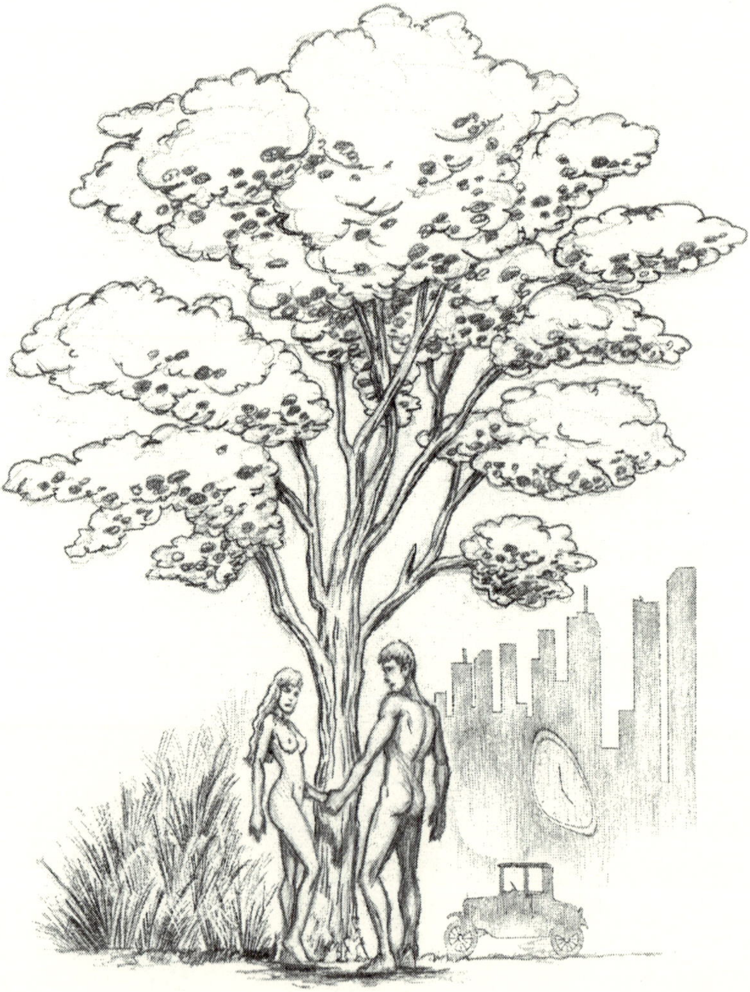

The garden of Eden
grew human-volition,
animals, plants, weeds, and trees.
The great Earth stretching evolution
of Earth in seas, and soils, and seeds.
Before preferences entered the picture with the
consciousness of infinitely separate 'you' vs. 'me.'

At that point in our evolution though
all things according to their unified natures
thrived on Earth free.
But the lone exception to the initial fractal freedom
was the fruit of that damned ego tree.
Because the knowledge of
potential 'goods' and potential 'evils'
would inevitably spread otherness
to the corners on the breeze.

But don't just trust me,
let's try an experiment.
Pay attention to your breathing...
Then to what your 'mind' will next foment?

(slow relaxed breath x3)

...My bet...
is that your next distracted thought
will be made up of some knowledge
of a longed for good or a resisted evil.
Or a preference leading to competing
with 'separate-selves', 'other' people.
A potential windfall, or a fear.
Professional ambitions or scares.
Enemies, friends, tacos, beers,
a new car, or better hair.

The game of egoic consuming
has become destructively redundant.
We've lost inherent grounding
to the storied life abundant.
Consciousness is rapidly being lost.
Our moments now just consist of a jumble
of compulsively anxious thoughts.
Of prides and fears,
or shoulds and aughts.
And Marketing...
as the new town preacher
promises meaning
in things we've bought.

But the planetary misery
that comes from humans
growing hell is the product
of the errant misconception
projecting 'otherness'
onto 'separate-selves'.
But the lesson taught
when Adam and Eve 'fell'*
was about forgotten ontological-Oneness
not assigning blame and moral-perils.

The expanse between pure experience...
and 'ego-consciousness'
is what was once called the fruit
of "the knowledge of good and evil".
The fruit made us forget...
That "it is fundamentally
in 'terms' of 'abstractions'
that we think."**
So said the late great Alan Watts.
So instead, I'll meet you in the Now.
Where we are more
than just our thoughts.

Since it is becoming increasingly clear
that in order for Earth to ever again be free.
We must again begin to see all things
as a co-operating 'Us'
not a competing 'you' vs. 'me'.

Or entropic otherness will eventually
boil off our seven-seas.
Ending Earth's story
in separated misery.

Unless mankind can now transcend
the fruit of the damned ego tree.

* *Genesis 3:1-11*
** *Alan W. Watts (1915-1973)*

27. My Generation

What is the role of a generation?
I was thinking all that through the other day.
And sort of thought it might be to enable
the next generation to thrive on their way.
But on their way to what?
...And in these times
first, we'd need to decide,
just what is our definition
of a well lived life?
And what does it look like
in these times to thrive?

I was thinking about my kids. Thriving!
All our children thriving vs. just surviving.
But our mass material consumption,
this current game...
My generation is being compulsively driven
by economic striving and illusory electronic fame.
What have our souls given up?
In modern-life's unconscious exchange?

There is a cost for our support
of damned power-systems.
As lives, souls, nature
are being fed into the engine.
Responsibility for the
technological-corporate takeover
of life itself falls to this generation.

Or for the next generation to thrive.
Or to achieve a good old' fashioned career
first, they'll have to bow down and accept shackles.
Prostrate before corporate gods out of fear.

Or risk somehow scratching a living off the land.
The price of freedom for future generations
may well be lean times, getting by, empty hands.

My generation's proof will be in our pudding,
it will be proved in the taste of our fruit.
Is what we are growing sweet or is it rotten?
Mother Earth seems to be screaming out
"rotten"! "Rotten to the bottom".

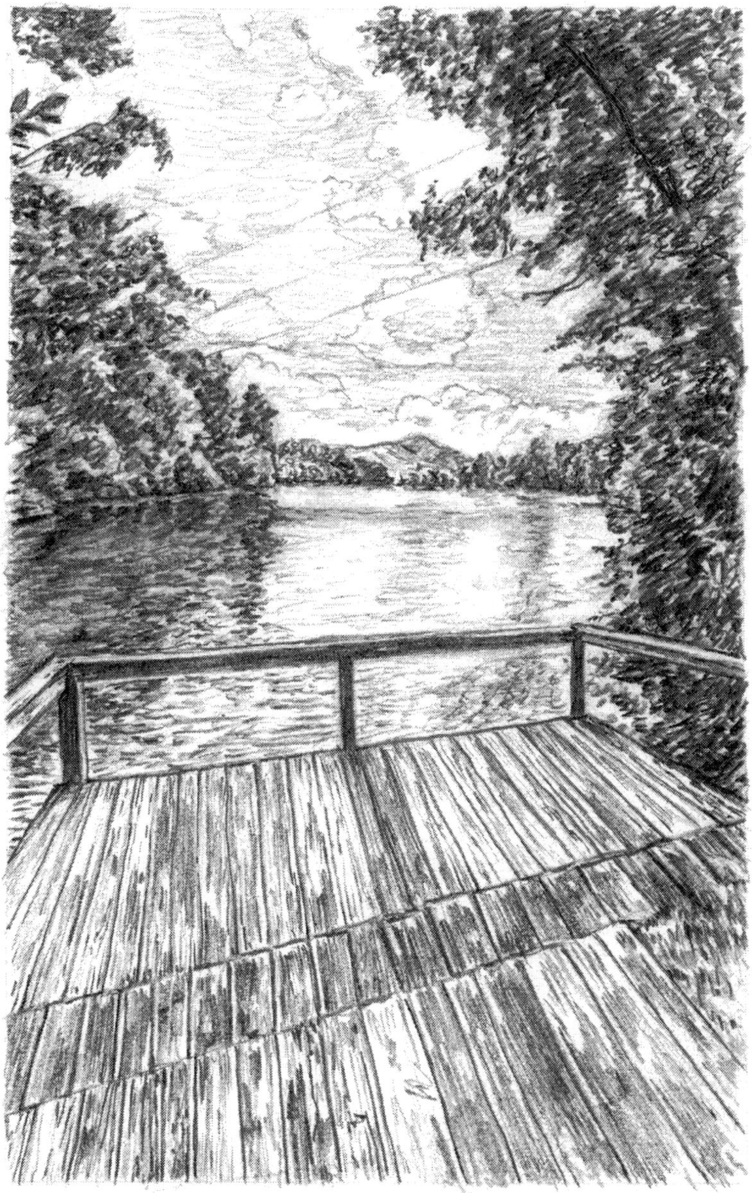

At this point... is what we're begetting
even worth getting?
Because what we're forgetting
is that comfort...
is not worth this trade!

So as my generation rolls over,
as our light turns into our shade.
We must sacrifice
and from Babylon
courageously un-couple.
We will leave future generations
Oneness...
or rubble.

28. COVID

I hear her upstairs coughing,
home from school on a Tuesday at noon.
I'm home too, instead of where I apparently "should be".
(Quote unquote) "in the Emergency room".

Instead, I'm in a recliner
alternating ice and heat on my back.
It is in a locked up in-tense defensive-spasm.
A mind-body reaction as if I'm under attack.
Before leaving work I just about fell to the floor.
I caught-myself on the frame of a door with a smack.
My complaints against this country's corporate overlords
have officially become a tumbledown stack.
Corporate grief has given me more than gray hairs.
There's also pain that comes along with their cares.

For starters, why are we still dealing with this virus?
A 'pandemic' that's been weaponized against us,
that's why this virus is still with us not behind us.

Thus, my daughter, is upstairs coughing.
And craving comfort via Chick Fil-A.
Life has thrown another challenge her way.
This time around it's COVID,
so, for my daughter... who has COVID, I pray.

America was once the pinnacle of innovation.
Before corporate media and politicians divided the nation
and began treating us people as pawns in their game.
Bartered over as fuel.
Or traded off as cheap meat.
Our divisions are now mass marketed
in the news, by politicians, into our streets.

Instead of a triumphant American
transcendence of a sickness.
We are eating ourselves in utter confusion,
consumed by this 'otherness' delusion.

But 'God'... once upon a time said,
"Let there Be".*
And somehow or other
what blew along,
was all this. You and me.

So why are we fighting each other about vaccines?
When the enemy is not us,
but ravenous, impersonal, corporate-machines.
Using tax funded profits to buy future decisions.
No longer just excessive pay,
opulent homes, and extravagant vacations.

Thus, our nation's corporate-politicians
have not given us a single
recommended at home treatment or
prevention protocol.
It's as if they're objective
is not our well-being at all.

Forget sharing preventative healthful living measures.
No, no, they just sell fear. Followed by injections.
Amp up a consuming competition over pleasures.
And shame all generic, inexpensive,
yet effective solutions.
So that the god of Pharma,
the god of 'Health'-care,
and the god of Science,
will become modern man's golden idols.

...Thus, my daughter is upstairs blowing her nose.
I'm confident she'll beat COVID like the rest of us Jones'
even though helpful treatment science
has been effectively silenced.
How best to help her???
None of us at home are allowed to know.
Our leaders are too busy
burning down the world
in exchange for a future,
they alone own.

For all the greed, all the power, all the thrones
they pump fear not health into our homes.
Censor freedom and censor knowledge
as our health… it endangers their game.

So, my daughter who has COVID is upstairs.
Guess our daughters
are more profitable stuck there.
Marketing targets
in their rooms with their pain.

*Genesis 1:1-31

29. Undying and Unborn

Could it ease the collective grind
of the collective mind to remember?
Remember that what 'I' see as 'I' is stardust...
become aware of itself.
'I' with my bluster and mistrust,
preferences, and lusts
have eternally spun into Being.
Now, I'm a food-formed body a husk.

And this shell, these cells, will melt back to the turf.
But awareness, consciousness,
is not bound to this Earth.
In truth what 'is' our center is eternal.
But separate egos are obsessed with forms.
And form is fundamentally finite.
But the Monad, the Divine-Self, the Christ,
remains undying and unborn.

Where "the knowledge of good and evil",*
where separate-self thinking takes Us.
Has dominated humanity, made Us
constricted not spacious.

Will 'thinking', will 'mind', will 'egos'
remain mankind's prison?
Or can we transcend the false narrative,
Become God's unified vision?
To see consciousness as shared Divinity
beyond just stardust with breath.
Is to admit we are the Creator...
of each moment we have left.

But if our collective consciousness
stays chained to separate 'I's.
Vacillating back and forth
between individual prides and moral slides
while consumption spins suffering
man-made hell multiplies.

As separate selves crave divides
we fuel the rising of tides.
And record cries from the skies.
Decay and suffering it seems have become
the ego's grand-prize.
But the separate 'I' is simply a disguise.

Fundamental Oneness
is what an infinite Cosmos implies.
To Be... loving awareness**
is Divinity realized.
Realizing Itself... through stardust with eyes.

Yet, "everything dies, baby... that's a fact.
But maybe everything that dies
some day comes back".***
The dance of God manifesting God
is the point! Not these temporal forms.
Remember. We are Christ...
Conscious as stardust
undying and unborn.

* *Genesis 2:9, 2:16-17*
** *Ram Dass, mantra (1931-2019)*
*** *Bruce Springsteen, "Atlantic City". Nebraska 1982*

30. The Precipice

Humanity... stands on the precipice.
Captive to the corporate appetite for profit.
Our insatiable consumption created the ledge
and now beckons us to jump off it.
We're held at the edge by collective in-action.
And media, politicians, and advertisers creating factions.

The devil of consumerism grins with each transaction,
knowing 'things' will never deliver satisfaction.
So more, more, more remains our collective re-action.
As we writhe in a frenzied egoic-spasm.
Within our full stomach's – fear breeds.
Scared egos brainwashed into greed for separate needs.

Life on separateness' edge
is about 'Me' to hell with 'We'.
Thus, We stay chained to the wheel.
As an excavator of progress digs round our feet.
Mother Earth is literally
sweating hurricanes as she overheats.

Our soil is being sacrificed before us.
Rich life-giving dirt is disappearing
faster than Earth's forests.
As the promises we built lives on
now fail us.
The transition to Oneness,
requires changes most courageous.

Because the behaviors and actions of today
have life itself shackled
to an existential ledge as prey.

Until once more we engage all 'others'
in and as unified presence
and turn this hell we've made…
back into heaven.

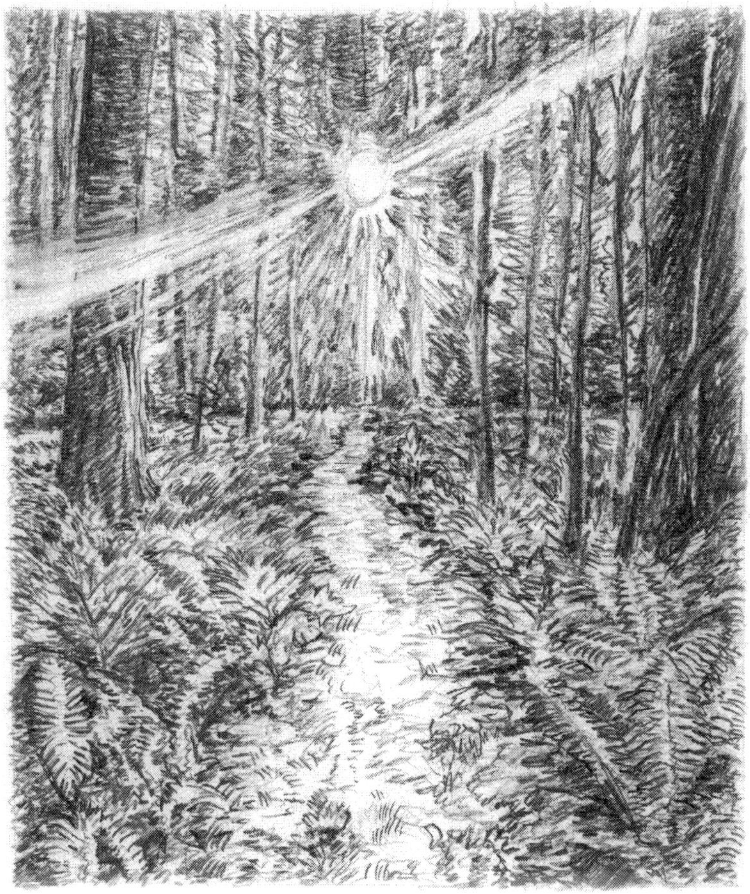

31. What If?

What if in the end – I wasn't let in
through the old pearly gates?
What if I didn't even get-a...
"Stand over there... sir, and wait"?
If this life of toil, this life of mine
did not measure up on the scales of the Divine?
Food stamp lines confused life... as a grind,
to a fragile young mind that now cannot unwind.
A life spent grappling for more.
From friends, to girls, to sports, to stores.
From money to pleasure to pride to my drawers.
I always seek the fight, whether it was needed or not.
Fights with those that I love, and those I've forgot.
Every person, every test, every instance of trying,
life became a treadmill of striving.
War-ing every challenge. On no one taking mercy.
To wake up at 40... asking "what's with all this hurry"?
But I now see what's the point.
I can see Just What matters.
And it's ending my bondage to preferences and rathers.

No longer seeking 'eternal life' by willing it so.
But Spirit – smiles at itself, because it knows, and I know.
That the path has been paved, victory already won.
'Eternal salvation' is accomplished.
And it will be done.

So set down preference,
seek Ye presence,
find God's eyes in this here place.
Smile, breath, Be!
"The kingdom of Heaven is within you".*
And your consciousness
did not manifest to 'rat-race'.

Instead, take a stroll with God
as the cool of the morn.
Just relax little striver,
the veil is already torn.
"Well done, good faithful Servant"**
...I pray that I hear...
So I'll meet moments
with the confidence of those words,
echoing love eternally in my ear.

* *Jesus of Nazareth, Matthew 10:7*
** *Jesus of Nazareth, Luke 19:17*

32. New Skin

I woke up one day and decided to change my skin.*
I'm sure that sounded crazy so I'll say it all again.
I woke up… one day and decided to change my skin.
Not as much my idea as that it grew out from within.

It seems new skin was required
because the old had become tired.
A frame of reference turned brittle
inside a paradigm too little.

Or picture this idea I am spitting
as an analogy like… knitting.
But the fabric's random where we're sitting
and the patches we are sewing are all ill-fitting.
Or how we eat and drink to hearty
when we're with friends or at a party.
Because a vice grows from a crutch
when we reach for it too much.
Ok… apologies for my ramble.
Thanks for dealing with that preamble.
While I get back to the bottom line
we need new skin to hold new wine.

Fresh capacity designed to hold a consciousness Divine.
I noticed a new consciousness...
Let's call that the new wine.
When I released the incessant fears
of an uncontrolled future space and time.
So old skin – I'll summarize as the egoic-mind.
And if I tried to contain this New
along with the egoic burdens I usually hold onto.
Then projected shadows I would spew,
and all my ends would come unglued.
So, I resolved to "just let go...
I woke up one day... and decided to kill my ego".**

To shed my old skin!
Now that's some ice that's thin!

To just let go.

As an exchange.

Of all I "could not hold onto.

And exchange it all, for a hope…

That lies beyond the blue".***

But as a child of this big-blue

That's a hard thing to do.

How do we shed the egoic mind?

Within this myth called space and time?

I can't lie. It is a constant struggle

to shift my awareness

from habitually imagined trouble.

But at the same time

this new wine

has been so freeing.

To finally live out

"In Christ we live and move and have our Being".****

---

* Jesus of Nazareth, Mark 2:21-22
** Sturgill Simpson, "Just Let Go" Metamodern Sounds in Country Music 2014.
*** Josh Garrels, "Beyond the Blue". Love and War and the Sea In Between 2011.
**** Acts 17:28

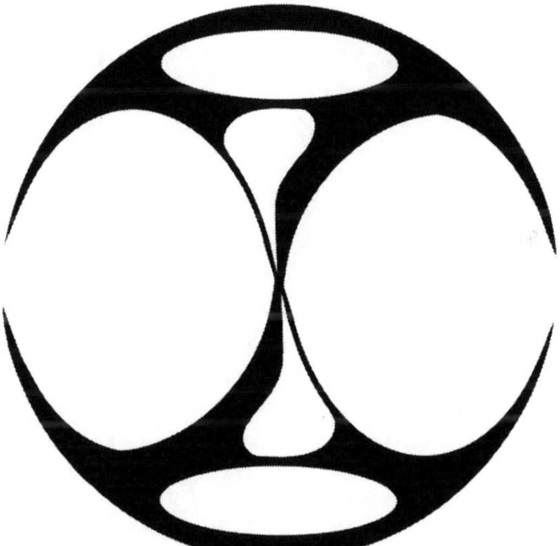

33. Polar Breeze

This thing we are doing.

This way that rules our day.

This curated rage we are consuming.

This spirit of enmity that leads our way.

It leads us far from freedom,

instead feeds us fear and tucks us in.

Because we are what is consuming us

consuming ourselves, from within.

The way that We are going,
the way we treat our fellow-selves.
Our culture has become a buffet of attachments,
and the collective ego is engorged.
Such a silly game we inflict on Us
squabbling over a preference scoreboard.

So, what then is our way forward?
What is the future we will co-create?
I believe one day it will be love…
flowering from oneness
within present moments.
Polar opposites masquerading as politics
manifests instead only hate.

Thus, the fruit of separate egos
the fruit of 'sin's' disease
is that I guess it should
feel this gut wrenching
as the hope of our 'nations',
blow away in a polar breeze.

34. This game we keep playing

The wages of 'otherness', we don't yet know.
But our shared future no longer comes slow.
Collectively what we are Becoming,
is how God falls
into form
like the snow.
God's self-emptying love.
Living-water. The Cosmic-sea.
Evolving in and as, You and Me.

And currently ego-consciousness
is driving this planet to its knees.
Multiplying suffering and injustice by the little threes.
Trash… may end up the legacy
left behind of Earth's trees.
We all know the adage – "sex-sells".

But I think the powerful would now disagree.
Otherness sells better than sex.
The selling of pride and protections has all the grease.

Yet somehow, in the inevitability of Love
I still believe.
One day we will all take a knee.
But on Earth, right now we're all losing.
Because this game we keep playing is not free.

35. Attachment

Strings come with things.
And things come with strings.
Why do they draw me so?
Yet to Be...
Is God in living
where the deer
and turkey go.

36. Our Destiny

Be quiet. Pay attention.
Without thinking notice breathing.
Maybe even watch,
as it changes how you're seeing.

Damnations
begot Nations,
who begot divides of our creation.
Christ-consciousness will eventually
beget a unification of our species.
But the question of our time remains,
how long will we wallow
in the ego's feces?

To the point of Life! Existence!
we act, as if we're blind.
We will be evolving toward a Divine destiny.
When presence transcends unconsciousness
and mankind is freed from our
conditioned self-seeking 'mind.'

Or right there – should my syntax have
again used the word 'ego'?
Or maybe right there used 'separate-self'?
Because our separate-successes and separate-protections
has humanity on the verge of massive insurrections.
Have we all just given in?
To social media and being mean?
Do we just so love our shackles,
chained in hypnosis to the more-machine?

Or could conscious breathing teach us Being?
Ontological Oneness is Our destiny
separation the-dream.

37. Everything is True

Everything... is true.
Well, I guess I did it again.
Start out with a statement shocking
just to circle back to it at the end.

Well, everything is true.
Truth can't be contained in just one view.
And the way I learned to find it
was to become willing to undo.
If it is...
its ultimate origin is God.
That's true of every-thing
from joy to suffering, humans to sod.
God is truth
is not limited to either perspects pole.
Our source cannot be contained,
but contains all that is inside the Whole.

Jesus, taught to worship in Spirit and in truth.
But it does not sound like Spirit
defending idolized-positions claw and tooth.
What is truth?

But 'Just What Is'.
If it is... it is true.
So don't let yourself be reduced,
identity captive to current views.

Defended group positions
and biases justify how egos feel.
But the All-Yes is all sides
and waits to meet us as the Real.

So yep, everything is true.
Every-thing spins from Creation's force.
So I'll meet you in the present moment
where we abide in the vine...*
Loves, Truths, Source.

*Jesus of Nazareth, John 15:4-5

38. A Practice

Join me in contemplating
the mystical words
"Let there Be"... They are heavy.
God, pouring out of an infinite levee.
Into a donut bubble of spinning energy –
we call the Universe.
But did 'Cosmic-Karma'
or 'Divine-Will' pour in first?

Which concept gets the credit
of first mover?
Where did we come from?
Form within the heart of life's Ruler?

Or does that not matter at all?
In the midst of Anthropos' great fall.
By the present moment
we just refuse to be held.
We're too busy creating
then habituating hell.

So, let's join in a practice
just now wherever you are.
Sit up straight on the couch.
Or pull over your car.
Come back to the peace…
that is this very moment,
relax eyes,
relax tension,
relax breath.
Feel Spirit in the wind
that fills your belly
then fills your chest.
Be here and be now in this moment
from in presence while "One, With, Life".*
And practice asking of your thoughts
is this thought even true?.?. **

The answer often
ends the tyranny of our fears.
The practice of present moments
lived freely
unites 'Life'
through new eyes and new ears.***

---

* *Eckhart Tolle, A New Earth: Awakening to Your Life's Purpose.*
** *Byron Katie, "The Work".*
*** *Ezekiel 12:2*

39. Transcending the Temporal

Fill your lungs.
Breathe in deep.
To your belly, breath is a reminder you are still here.
Still experiencing, this side of death's sleep.
Presence to this present moment
always births understandings never fears.
In actuality fear too often is imagined,
the ego whispering otherness in our ears.
Into black mirrors our culture casts spells
weaving myths that our plans keep us well.

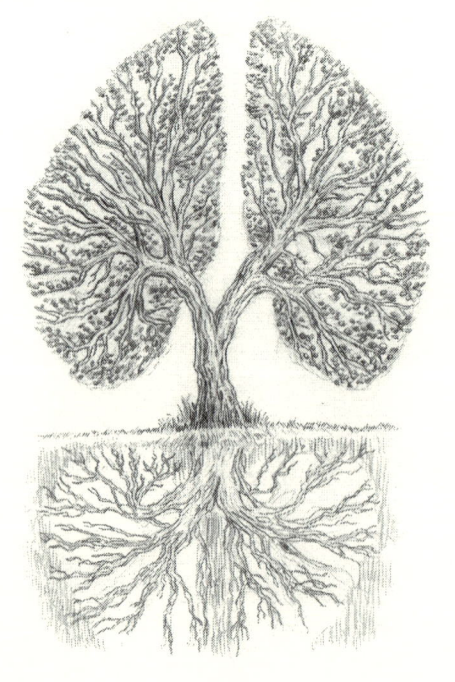

Yet, each moment is a fractal of potential.
When we join into the now's dance.
Let go of the mud you're dressed in it's a rental.
Your 'I' my 'me' is not the point it's a trance.
The eternal stretches out as life's crossroads.
Good and evil, Just What Is, manifests the I AM.
Christ Consciousness is the path of loving awareness.
Kenotic exchange not protections and plans.

While ego consciousness bows down
before the idol of protections.
Tribalizes opposing ideologies
and calls them elections.
While corporations sell colored plastic
and pills for erections,
more comfort, more couture, more confections…
Thus, humanity drifts off
dreaming of temporal distractions.

But one day,
I believe we'll wake up to Oneness. To Purpose.
Human consciousness
will unclench,
will breathe,
will one day,
transcend waring ego's
and divided factions.

40. The Sam's Wholesale Church

It seems like a lot of people
have stopped going to church.
Instead on Sunday's
they all go to Sam's...
Piling in there in all
shapes, colors, and sizes,
pouring out of trucks,
classic-cars, and minivans.

...If our 'God'...
is from what we derive our meaning.
Then bulk consuming
and material-goods competing
is now what draws in the
congregants streaming.

As we crowd-fund
plastic water bottle pollution.
And keep the masses satiated
and sleepily producing.
But this exponential producing
seems to me to be end times inducing.

Because 'meaning' is now sought in 'stuff'.
Stuff emerging from merciless
environmental abusing.
As separate-ego's bow...
bow down before the gods of consuming.

What is the future
we are growing from this now?
What is the consciousness grown
from material goods
as the object of our bows?

The world's foundations
sure seem to be
getting pretty shaky.
Meaning is disappearing
as quickly as
rotisserie-chickens lately.
Because our Sunday sermons
now come from the sample lady.

41. The Threshing Floor

I just saw an image...
somewhere inside my brain.
It was a large stone inside a circle,
a whipping post for the releasing of grain.

A hulk of stone was positioned just at the center.
Like a saddle horn for the threshing of wheat,
purposed to test resolve,
of grains that strong and grains that weak.

I'm not exactly sure? Just why I saw it?
What this image was intended to convey?
All I can think is that it was an analogy.
Like a parable... for the meaning of these days.

Somewhere along the way to today,
we decided the point of life
was to live like kings.
Demanding,
more comfort,
more pleasures,
more things.

What have these recent times been
but a threshing floor?
Freeing humanity's seed
from Our bondage
from attachments,
unconscious desires
and cults of more.

It seems humanity is being flailed
in order to free Us,
from scarcity-consciousness
and endless economic-wars.

42. Humorous Diversity

Have you ever contemplated Earth's cosmic birth?
I mean really, really think about it?
Consider all the crazy things,
on their own that just grow
up and out of it.
How in the Cosmos…
in the mind melting immensity?
Did We grow Earth
filled with such a humorous diversity.

Take an example like any
old nature show on the tele.
Or better yet take a field trip
stroll through an
Appalachian wooded valley.
Or how about the example
of tropical birds.
With their crazy shapes,
crazy colors,
crazy dances for their girls.
Or how… somehow inevitably
natural shapes end up in curls.

From the mosses to the mountains,
to the sprouting up of men.
It's a reminder it is all One.
We grew from Earth's soil
since who knows when.

Earth is not filled
with diverse enemies.
It's filled with humor.
Filled with friends.

43. The Universe is Breathing Me

I am not so much breathing
as the Universe seems to Be,
breathing me.
I don't have to attempt to will it,
the Cosmic Christ's outpouring fills it.

Thus, to be breathed is grace,
it is a gift that's given free.
The universal offsetting
balance is also grace
always yin, always yang,
humans breathing, breathing trees.

Take a moment, watch yourself be breathed.
In and out
breath's unrelenting tide.
Makes you wonder what is the point
of consciousness' breath-less ride?

It will not remain us forever clinging
to personas, to egos, to separate 'I's.
But in Being breathed... as a grace
like Eckhart says, we're "One With Life".*

As we consciously perceive the Universe breath,
we form a relationship with Spirit.
And join the dance...
of Just What Is.
Realizing not in our thoughts
but in loving awareness,**
we are fulfilled.

* *Eckhart Tolle, A New Earth: Awakening to Your Life's Purpose..*
** *Ram Dass, mantra (1931-2019)*

44. Divided Lines

Religion... should be how we live.
Not the structured belief system
with which we identify.
So, it is past-time we all start asking
why establishment faiths
refuse to transcend the script.
Of defended agreements
and divided lines?

Selling fears, followed closely,
by systemic rules to then live by.
Why is modern religion still focused on words?
On what 'they' believe, and what 'we' believe?
Not on creating a new Earth,
but defending idolized-ideologies.

Power systems of competing egos
paying blood taxes on their greed.
Scoring eternal-points
through very sweet external charity
produces capital-R 'Religion'.
Not surrendered hearts.
But divisions of 'me'-over.
Our way over all 'others'
who don't quite agree.

All consumed by precise wording
dividing who is "in"... and who is "out".
But not enough contemplation about
how religions of divisions...
is turning out.

45. 'It'... Is Happening

'Christ', (the word for God's self-emptying) is happening.
Now.
'It' is – happening now.
So, what would Jesus do???
About... 'It'?
That situation in your home. Or with your friends.
Or another struggle against-the 'others'
we separate from and then contend?

Only the Christ, would not by now have come unglued!
With our attitudes and our behaviors
The way we 'other' both our planet and our neighbors.
Far afield from Jesus' points mankind has moved.

We often miss His story's arc.
The plot behind Mary's broken heart.
Why He did just what He did.
Why He said just what He said.
And why the lesson had to conclude
with Him hanging up there, dead?

Can I dare..? Can I dare?
To wonder out loud,

what into these times,
what He might say?
...Maybe something like
Hey, you know that separate-ego you tend to live from?
Well dig it out by the roots and throw it away.
Or would He speak up for His planet?
Before our consumption finally damns-it?

Or tell us our power structures,
and our pursuits of 'success',
are just the sparkle on the bodice
of the antichrist's wedding dress.
I believe Jesus Christ lived that life for more than this.
Died that death for more than this.
The "knowledge of good and evil"
became our Judas,
when the ego claimed us with a kiss.

When Jesus multiplied His presence
by sending out His twelve.
He told them to take nothing,
leave all that distracts back on the shelves.
Because the point His life seemed to make...
was that the point of life attachments take,

as worries and clinging's slowly grate
away at our Divinity and compromise our Center.
We toil away our lives,
and the kingdom of heaven we fail to enter.

Bound to old wood and rusty nails
I hear a distant voice, a silent wail.
It says "Take courage
'it' is… 'I'… so do not be afraid."*
Our Father's love it is inevitable
And heaven is the road We together pave.

So, 'Christ' meets us.
As here and now.
In and as this very moment
where we will finally see
that 'it' is all the 'Christ',
even when 'it' nailed 'Him' to a tree.
Then as promised
went on ahead
and waits right here…
in Galilee.**

Jesus of Nazareth: Matthew 14:27
** Jesus of Nazareth: Mark 14:28

46. The Physicist's Key

Physicists are presently seeking
a fundamental pattern of division.
They postulate if they can find
the fractal pattern that grows division.
Humanity could escape the
earthbound three-dimensional prison
in which we're living.

As a key to a lock,
this understanding could birth creation.
But with such power over things
would we end power-systems?
...Or just remake them?

I for one, do not think we are ready,
as in the sorta...
"this is why we can't have
nice things" kinda way.
Watch for yourself, on tonight's news.
Watch us accuse, watch us bruise,
watch us judge, watch us weigh,
watch us peruse the divided highlights
of yet another divided day.

It's a spinning fractal vision of division.
Souls torn asunder as internal combustion.
We've become the fuel.
And we're being driven into their engine.
Power-systems preach "worry"!
About "other"!
And bow down to power, just don't awaken.
Just focus in on this year's must have 'things'.
Things, we are trading Earth away in making...
Unconscious profit chasing, and social faking.
With Corporate-Politicians
behind the wheel
we race to hell...
and we're not braking.

Maybe this pattern,
of fractal division… is our ticket?
Maybe we sink the full court shot
of saving Earth.
Maybe we brick it?
That kind of math though
is well above my limit.
Instead, I'll work with my moments,
try to be present to those I'm given.

To bring unguarded loving awareness to life
has been the key since the beginning.
So, I'll meet you in the now
forgiving 'thisness'
in fractals spinning.

47. There is something made of Love up next.

It has got to just feel mental
to stare into your own impending death.
Death's goodbye, sure makes us fearful.
The abyss opening up after breath.

What is next? Will we float or will we stand?
Is Someone waiting reaching out for our hand?
Will we sink into fear?
Will we breathe into faith?
Or will we hide in depression's dark lands?

Because my time at the precipice will soon arrive.
Human life is so cosmically brief.
Or should I've said comically brief?
So before God draws this soul from its sheath.
I'll speculate. Take a guess
before my grave wear's a wreath.

There is something made of Love... up next.
And there are things here,
that make me sad to think to miss.
Marriages and births to be witnessed.

Laughing at friends when they trip.

The electricity of a kiss.

Picking up fruit, drawing it close, taking a whiff.

But there is something made of Love up next.
And there has never been 'nothing' – anywhere.
In the same way that steel pouring out of a foundry
is sub-atomically still mostly air.

Matter is just a field of perceived spatial boundaries.
And yet there is no emptiness anywhere.
Out to the farthest corner of the Cosmos
nothing... nothing just plain old does not exist.
There is Spirit, movement, potential in the quantum.
In the fractal field of the sub-atomic there is no bottom.
The light after the darkness insists,
it is Love. It is infinite. It is Heaven.

There is something made of Love up next.
Where Our purpose will be manifest everywhere.
It is the land of Union. Communion.
Where we'll Be... after laying down cares.

Though the flight from here
into eternal reunion.
It does not come with a map.
So, it falls to each of Us
to smile, let go, release.
"God is Love"*
and will fill in our cracks.
Provide courage, faith, vision where we lack.
So, as you fly Home
don't turn and look over your back.
Your circuitous flight into the singularity of Love
will always remain eternally on track.

* 1 John 4:8

48. God Saves Through Self Emptying

Sitting in my daily
morning meditation
I caught myself
in a forced smiling frown.
The kind I have to will up
to resist tears that promise relief
by escaping my eyes
and falling onto the ground.

I learned right before I sat down
of the passing-away of a visionary.
The last day. Of the great teacher Thay.
Christ Consciousness just lost a giant.

Thich Nhat Hanh,
the friend of Thomas Merton
and Martin Luther King Jr.
Thay, last night passed away.
But he's now
being called by his true names.*

In this morning's sit,
came to me a rephrasing.
A Name. As another way to say.
"God Saves – Through Our Self Emptying"
is "Jesus-Christ" reinterpreted today.
What else does the name above all names say?
But to convey kenotic love
in sheer dramatic display?

An Incarnation spent as moments of loving awareness
poured out upon Just What Was.
With no account for separate preferences cost.
Just smiling, breathing, Being.
All the way to the old rugged cross.

Thay, through mindful breathing
somehow tamed the tiger within.*
The Holy Spirit moved him to Interbeing.*
Thay's life was breathed as peace in every step.*
So, his passing left me sort of reeling
wondering if there are any more giants left?

This planet is desperate for meaning.
We need a modern day
Ram Dass,
a Buddha,
a Jesus,
a Thay,
Because our ears are all stopped up with profits.
Materialistic-consumers busy lining our pockets.
Tuning out and killing off all the prophets.
That Just What Was
in sacrificial love sent our way.

Who is left?
To teach us to live in the here and the now?*
In the turmoil of Heaven growing wild?
So that the next twenty-four-brand-new-hours*
will be conscious moments
chock full of loving smiles.

Who will tell us the next time
we lose our conscious smile
to remember the dandelion has it?*
And God saves through self-emptying trials.

* *Thich Nhat Hanh – Various books, writings, quotes, and teachings.*

49. Consciousness and...

Breath at last will one day cease.
Consciousness and...
pass on, into peace.

When from there
we look back on this life
will we mourn lives,
we traded for trife?

Possessions, things,
our treasured baggage,
houses, cars, and clothes,
remembered as garbage.

Consciousness and...
will 'Be' in 'heaven above'
Consciousness and...
present moments
magnetic Love.

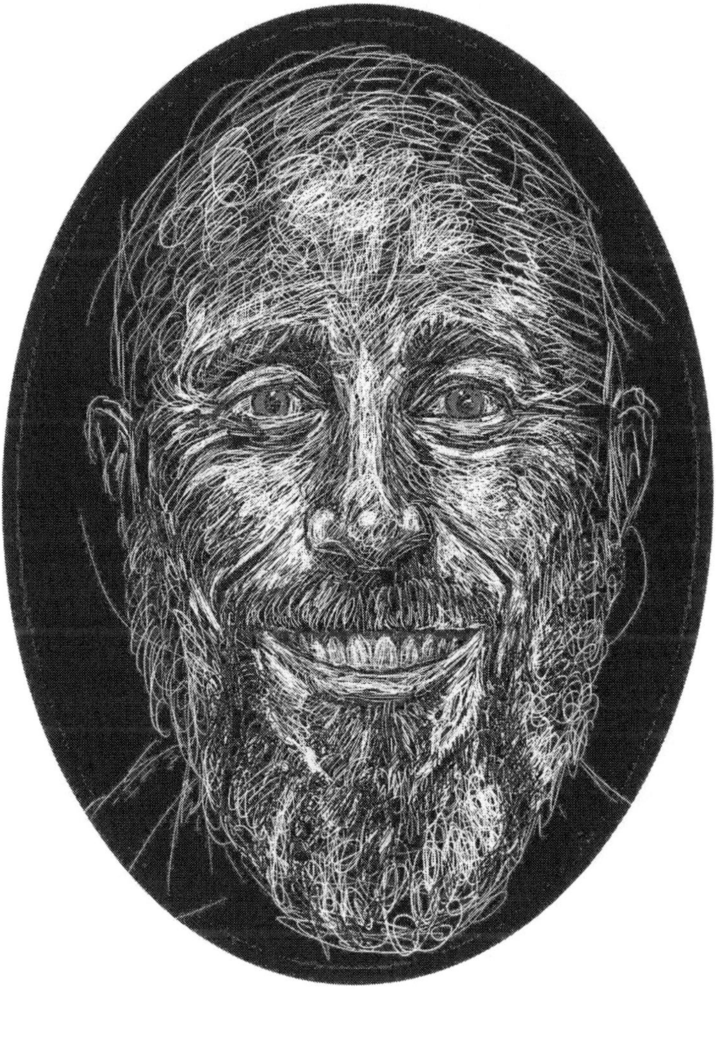

50. Miracles

Do you want to hear about a miracle?
And I don't mean a miracle that's satirical
but literal. Even though as typical
it will come out a little lyrical.

First of all, it's a miracle
if these words have reached… you.
These words've had a bumpy ride
on their way to meet you.
If you have read this far, that is miraculous!
These words became vernaculous.

Along the way, though these words
will have transcended a legion of opposition.
They came to me like a hurricane.
A veritable obstriction of diction.

But that's not really the miracle
I sat down to write about.
But a little extra I must acknowledge
a gift of God, I must point out.

The miracle I wish to speak of is a hope
From dystopia it's our way out.
We are not yet damned!!!
Mankind is not yet over a barrel!
A harmonious, fulfilled, free, humanity...
The singularity of Love is... just inevitable.
Though the path from here to there
may take hard years to escape these perils.

Because power-systems now mandate domination.
As human hostages now live in virtual prisons
held-behind electronic bars.
Installed by corporations who've purchased our nations.
In my country our cages are adorned with pretty trinkets.
The miracle I speak of though is about how we do life
and that blessed day when we rethink it.

Rethink it and realize the fact,
that all these separate preferences that fill our brains,
are just well-crafted games...
Games that promise joys and deliver chains.
Custom built to maintain control and profit
shackling the world to more of the same.

Thus, humanity staggers drunk...
drunk on the froth of assigning blame.
Prisoners to preference,
plastic-egos, and electronic fame.
Though cultural conformity
and cancelations
will not remain for eternity
the borders of life's frame!

It will not be this way forever,
so don't succumb to their lies of "never".

The times we live in are ripe with child.
Pregnant, with the miracle of a future birth.
A miraculous arising up of 'Heaven'.
Christ Conscious Us re-making Earth.

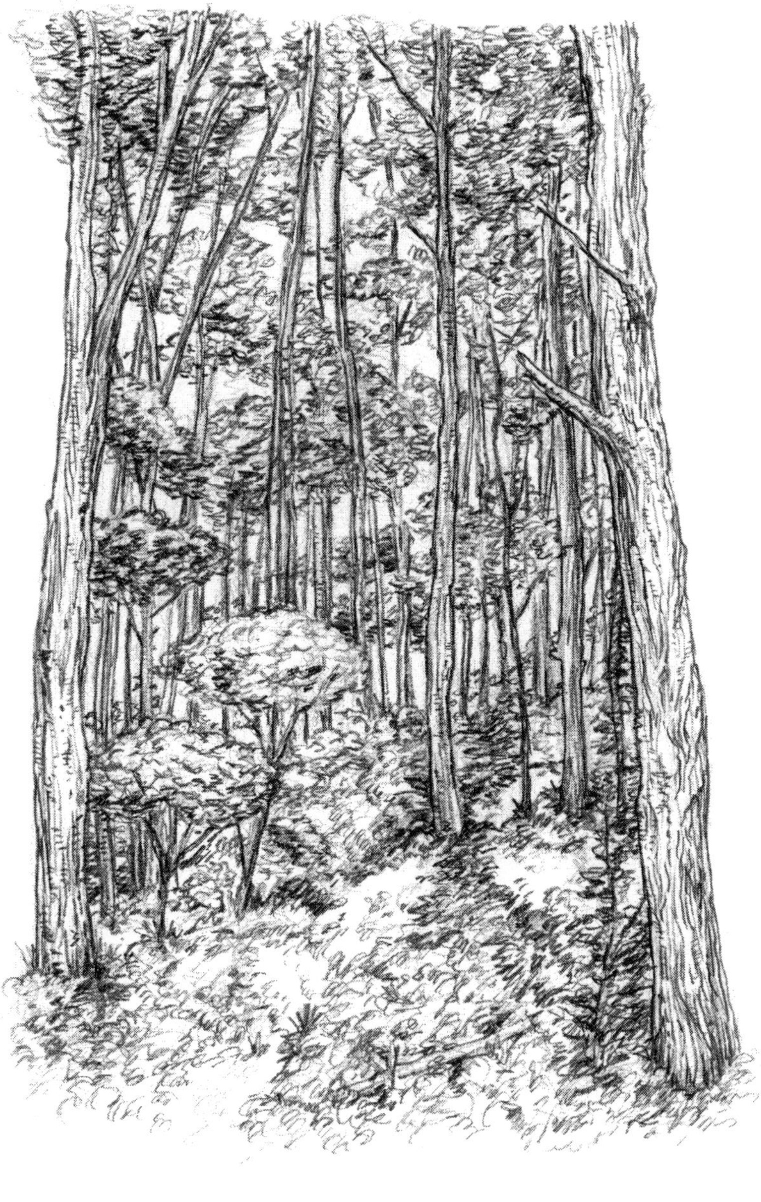

51. Home Grown

There is no such thing as the future!
...ok I came right out and said it.
The future is a myth, so is the past.
Present moments are all we've ever known.

That means 'Heaven' is here and now.
Not out there...
somewhere-else, some-place, some-time unknown.
I don't think we are waiting on admittance
beyond some clouded throne.
It must already be taking shape
as what it is destined to one day be.

The inevitable singularity of Love...
What Must Be will one day set us free.

But if we stay caught up in separate egos, and within
thought patterns spin.
Imagined sufferings and pleasures
increasingly become our focus
as games of preferences, we try to win.
The egoic "fruit of the
knowledge of good and evil"*
has grown like this since the garden of Eden.

But, then Jesus Christ came along and told Us,
"the kingdom of heaven is inside you".**
But I'm not sure we know just what that means.
Could it be that from the
quantum of conscious moments?
We actively manifest
what Heaven will be?

And if we can lay aside separate preferences.
We'd all find another way from the inside.
From a place called Love
that feels like Home.
Heaven will be home grown.

*Genesis 2:16-17
**Jesus of Nazareth: Luke 17:20-21; Matthew 10:7

52. Into the Now

I for One...
want to 'Be' present.
To shake the dust off 'Just What Is'.

Because here and now
God is calling for our presence.
Like a smiling
childhood Friend.

And this Friend
has all the good toys.
New eyes,
new ears,
a burden light,
and a big smile
...just like a child!
Eternity is made-up of Our moments
so we're growing 'Heaven' wild.

And We human beings,
We have the capacity
to consciously create it.

We know now
thoughts create forms.
We each manifest
as lives march forward.
Jesus Christ knew
something we've forgotten
and into the now,
His life,
Love poured.

EPILOGUE

Why the hell are we now perfuming trash bags?

Come on now.
Are you telling me that
on self-destruction
we are just so hell bent.
We compulsively
multiply consumerism's
chemical footprint.
By mindlessly destroying
with all our toying
Earth's environment.
We show no
respect for our home.
And we're overdue
with Earth's rent.
I wish I could end this one hopeful
be more song less lament.
But we are trading away
the only habitable planet
we even know exists.
In exchange for trash-bags
now featuring a
"Fresh Clean"
chemical scent.

Humanity looks to have ordered hell...
and added on super-sizing.
We're spending our last days
cooking up chemicals for
refuse-stench disguising.
At least the future smell of
the dead planet will be
slightly less putrefying.
Because marketing companies
now make the trash bags
full of some shit that's
"odor-neutralizing".

And yet...
From the quantum of individual
self-sacrificial decisions
hope against hope is arising.
So, I'll hang up this pen
stop wasting time philosophizing.

> "He who travels far will often see things
> far removed from what he believed was Truth.
> When he talks about it in the fields at home,
> he is often accused of lying,
> for the obdurate people will not believe."
> - Hermann Hesse, Journey to the East (1877-1962)

www.intothenow.org

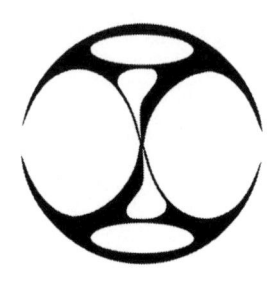

ACKNOWLEDGEMENTS

How can I thank those closest to me? To my children, my wife, our parents, and our larger family unit I give thanks for your patience with me as this book came together amidst the living of our life. Thanks to my friends and family of all shapes, colors, sizes, (and belief systems) – You make life worth living, I thank you for who You Are.

For the beautiful visual creations of Isaac Stone I stand in awe. You can find him on Instagram at Isaac.w.stone and support his work through Patreon et.al.

Many thanks to Mitch and Marissa McGarry with MayPop media who turn visions into realities. To the magical and talented Jorja Green I say namaste. And endless gratitude to both Alison Deadman and Ryan Fair for the grace they showed in helping me limp across the finish line. Shalom. Thanks to Nicole Melanson for her contribution to my process. Thanks to Dr. Jesse Graves, Allison Winters, and Nathan Wampler for their assistance.

I offer thanks to the multitude of friends who contributed to this journey in their unique ways. Including the late great author and philosopher Dr. John Francis Nash who contributed his wisdom, friendship, and advice over tea. To Ethan Magness, Ben Lee, Andrew Ford, Yvette Bryan, Darby Dickenson, Matt Osborne, and the fields and forests who served as my spiritual community I say thank you.

Credits from afar are owed to the inspiring thought leaders who were friends to this lonely seeker walking a lonely path – many thanks to; Joe Rogan, Duncan Trusell, Aubrey Marcus, James Finley, Kirsten Oates, Thomas Merton, Wim Hof, St. Teresa of Avila, Thich Nhat Hanh, Richard Rohr, Brie Stoner, Paul Swanson, Trevor Hall, IN-Q, Paul Chek, Boyd Varty, Ram Dass, Alan Watts, Guigo II, The Author of the Cloud of Unknowing, Eckhart Tolle, Dr. Steven Greer, Alice Bailey, Dion Fortune, Peter Crone, St. Francis of Assisi, J. Krishnamurti, Mooji, Rumi, Bob Marley, Sadhguru, David Goggins, Russel Brand, Dr. Joe Dispenza, Byron Katie, Charles Eisenstein, Tania Harris, Dr. Zach Bush, to my Christian friends from First Christian Church and Beaverdale Baptist and to the forgotten multitude who will spring to mind as soon as this book is published... I offer my thanks for your influence and your service unto the almighty 'Just What Is'.

Made in the USA
Columbia, SC
27 March 2023

831c87f5-cda2-4127-b7a2-5e1c1a74f223R01